U.S. PRESIDENTS

MYTHS OR FACTS?

MYTHS AND FACTS ABOUT JOHN F. KENNEDY

EZRA E. KNOPP

PowerKiDS press

Published in 2024 by The Rosen Publishing Group, Inc.
2544 Clinton Street, Buffalo, NY 14224

First Edition

Editor: Greg Roza
Book Design: Michael Flynn

Photo Credits: Cover Werkat/Shutterstock.com; (series background) Azamatovic/Shutterstock.com; p. 5 https://commons.wikimedia.org/wiki/File:TheKennedyFamily1.jpg; p. 7 https://commons.wikimedia.org/wiki/File:Kfc2073p_crop.jpg; p. 9 https://commons.wikimedia.org/wiki/File:USS_PT-105.jpg; p. 11 https://en.wikipedia.org/wiki/File:President_Kennedy_-_signing_Cuba_Quarantine_Proclamation.gif; p. 13 courtesy of Library of Congress; p. 15 https://commons.wikimedia.org/wiki/File:President_Kennedy_inaugural_address_(color).jpg; p. 17 https://commons.wikimedia.org/wiki/File:President_John_F._Kennedy_Speaks_at_Free_University_in_Berlin,_Germany_JFKWHP-ST-C230-18-63.jpg; p. 19 https://commons.wikimedia.org/wiki/File:President_greets_Peace_Corps_Volunteers._White_House,_South_Lawn._-_NARA_-_194180.jpg; p. 20 Charlie Hutton/Shutterstock.com.

Library of Congress Cataloging-in-Publication Data

Names: Knopp, Ezra E., author.
Title: Myths and facts about John F. Kennedy / Ezra E. Knopp.
Description: [Buffalo, New York] : PowerKids Press, [2024] | Series: U.S. presidents : myths or facts? | Includes bibliographical references and index.
Identifiers: LCCN 2023034880 (print) | LCCN 2023034881 (ebook) | ISBN 9781499444117 (library binding) | ISBN 9781499444100 (paperback) | ISBN 9781499444124 (ebook)
Subjects: LCSH: Kennedy, John F. (John Fitzgerald), 1917-1963–Juvenile literature. | Presidents–United States–Biography–Juvenile literature. | United States–Politics and government–1961-1963–Juvenile literature.
Classification: LCC E842.Z9 K62 2024 (print) | LCC E842.Z9 (ebook) | DDC 973.922092 [B]–dc23/eng/20230803
LC record available at https://lccn.loc.gov/2023034880
LC ebook record available at https://lccn.loc.gov/2023034881

Manufactured in the United States of America

IA Compliance Information: Batch #CWPK24. For Further Information contact Rosen Publishing at 1-800-237-9932.

CONTENTS

EARLY LIFE

John Fitzgerald Kennedy (often called JFK) was the second of nine children born to multimillionaire businessman Joseph Patrick Kennedy and his wife, Rose Fitzgerald Kennedy. The Kennedys were well-known in Massachusetts. Both of Kennedy's grandfathers were involved in state politics.

The Kennedys were a wealthy, famous family. They've long been known for their wealth and **philanthropy**. JFK and his brothers and sisters all went on to some form of fame. Several became politicians.

IT'S A FACT!

JFK'S YOUNGER SISTER EUNICE KENNEDY SHRIVER WAS A PHILANTHROPIST AND SOCIAL **ACTIVIST**. SHE FOUGHT FOR THE RIGHTS OF PEOPLE WITH **INTELLECTUAL** DISABILITIES AND FOUNDED THE SPECIAL OLYMPICS IN 1968.

THIS PHOTOGRAPH FROM 1931 SHOWS THE KENNEDY FAMILY IN HYANNIS PORT, MASSACHUSETTS. THE YOUNGEST CHILD, EDWARD "TED" KENNEDY, WASN'T YET BORN. THE DOG'S NAME WAS BUDDY!

MYTH OR FACT?

KENNEDY WAS RARELY SICK.

MYTH

Born May 29, 1917, Kennedy had numerous illnesses throughout his life. As a child, he suffered from whooping cough, measles, and chicken pox. Before he was even three years old, JFK spent about a month in a hospital with scarlet fever. He almost died.

Health issues would continue to be a problem for JFK his entire life. However, he loved sports and pranks. He injured his back while playing football for Harvard in college. The injury was a source of pain for the rest of his life.

IT'S A FACT!

IN 1947, DOCTORS TOLD KENNEDY THAT HE HAD ADDISON'S DISEASE, WHICH PREVENTS THE BODY FROM MAKING CHEMICALS CALLED HORMONES THAT IT NEEDS TO FUNCTION. KENNEDY HAD SO MANY BAD ILLNESSES THAT HE RECEIVED **LAST RITES** THREE TIMES BEFORE EVEN BECOMING PRESIDENT!

EVEN THOUGH HE WAS OFTEN IN PAIN OR ILL, KENNEDY HAD A VERY ACTIVE CHILDHOOD. THIS PICTURE FROM 1926 SHOWS A YOUNG JOHN KENNEDY WHILE HE ATTENDED A PRIVATE SCHOOL IN MASSACHUSETTS.

MILITARY HERO

MYTH OR FACT?

DUE TO HIS ILLNESSES, KENNEDY DID NOT MAKE A NOTABLE IMPACT WHILE SERVING IN THE U.S. NAVY DURING WORLD WAR II.

MYTH

After he graduated from Harvard in 1940, Kennedy tried to **enlist** in the U.S. Army, but he wasn't accepted because of his back injury. After strengthening his back with exercises, Kennedy enlisted in the U.S. Navy. He became an **intelligence officer**.

Once the United States entered World War II in 1941, Kennedy requested active duty in the South Pacific. He later became the commander of a patrol torpedo (PT) boat. In 1943, his boat was sunk by a Japanese ship. Although he was injured, Kennedy saved two other injured soldiers from drowning.

JFK COMMANDED A PT BOAT THAT LOOKED JUST LIKE THIS ONE.

MYTH OR FACT?

WHILE SHIPWRECKED ON AN ISLAND DURING WORLD WAR II, KENNEDY USED A COCONUT SHELL TO ESCAPE.

FACT

After their boat was destroyed, Kennedy ordered the other soldiers to swim to an island 3 miles (4.8 km) away. Kennedy helped one of the injured men reach the island. They lived on coconuts for days.

After moving to another nearby island, the soldiers met some local people in a canoe. These men were Coastwatchers, part of a network of spies who worked for the **Allies**. Kennedy carved a message into a coconut shell and asked the men to deliver it to U.S. forces on a nearby island. They were rescued soon after.

IT'S A FACT!

BECAUSE OF HIS BRAVERY AND SELFLESS ACTS, KENNEDY EARNED THE NAVY AND MARINE CORPS MEDAL AND A PURPLE HEART. KENNEDY WAS ALSO AWARDED SEVERAL OTHER MEDALS.

JFK KEPT THE COCONUT SHELL! HE DISPLAYED IT ON HIS DESK IN THE OVAL OFFICE WHILE HE SERVED AS PRESIDENT.

POLITICAL PATH

MYTH OR FACT?

KENNEDY GAVE HIS POLITICAL SALARIES TO CHARITY.

FACT

After the war, Kennedy pursued a political career. In 1946, he was elected to the U.S. House of Representatives. He also served in the U.S. Senate from 1953 to 1960. He was both popular and effective. His policies focused on social services, affordable rent, higher wages, and better working conditions.

Kennedy refused to accept a salary as a politician. He gave his salary to charities including the Boy Scouts and Girl Scouts of America, the United Negro College Fund, and the Cuban Families Committee.

KENNEDY WAS A U.S. CONGRESSMAN FOR SIX YEARS, A U.S. SENATOR FOR EIGHT YEARS, AND U.S. PRESIDENT FOR JUST UNDER THREE YEARS. THE TOTAL AMOUNT OF MONEY HE GAVE TO CHARITY DURING THIS TIME WAS ABOUT $500,000.

MYTH OR FACT?

KENNEDY WAS THE YOUNGEST PERSON TO BECOME A U.S. PRESIDENT.

MYTH

In 1961, at the age of 43, Kennedy became the youngest person *elected* to the office of U.S. president. However, he wasn't the youngest president ever. Theodore Roosevelt became president at age 42. He was vice president for President William McKinley. When McKinley was **assassinated** in 1901, Roosevelt took over.

Kennedy had very little time as president—just two years and 10 months. Only six other past presidents spent less time in office: Millard Fillmore, Gerald Ford, Warren G. Harding, Zachary Taylor, James A. Garfield, and William Henry Harrison.

DURING HIS **INAUGURATION** IN JANUARY 1961, KENNEDY FAMOUSLY STATED: "ASK NOT WHAT YOUR COUNTRY CAN DO FOR YOU-ASK WHAT YOU CAN DO FOR YOUR COUNTRY."

MYTH OR FACT?

PRESIDENT KENNEDY ONCE CALLED HIMSELF A "JELLY-FILLED DOUGHNUT" DURING A SPEECH IN BERLIN, GERMANY.

MYTH

The era after World War II, known as the Cold War, was a time of unease between the United States and the Soviet Union. In 1961, the Soviet Union built a wall in Berlin, Germany, separating their **communist**-controlled East Berlin from the democratically controlled West Berlin.

In 1963, President Kennedy visited West Berlin and spoke out against **oppression**. He said, *"Ich bin ein Berliner,"* which means "I am a Berliner," or someone from Berlin. In some places, "berliner" means a jelly-filled doughnut!

IT'S A FACT!

MANY YEARS AFTER HIS SPEECH, A RUMOR STARTED THAT KENNEDY CALLED HIMSELF A JELLY-FILLED DOUGHNUT, BUT THIS IS FALSE! IT'S A RUMOR THAT WAS SUPPORTED BY MANY MAJOR NEWS ORGANIZATIONS, SUCH AS THE *NEW YORK TIMES*, FOR YEARS.

TODAY, THE AREA WHERE KENNEDY MADE HIS SPEECH IS NAMED JOHN F. KENNEDY PLATZ. PLATZ IS THE GERMAN WORD FOR "PLACE."

MYTH OR FACT?

KENNEDY CREATED THE PEACE CORPS.

FACT

Kennedy was only president for just under three years before he was assassinated. During this short time, Kennedy did as much as he could to help people around the world. Kennedy proposed the **Civil Rights Act** shortly before his death in 1963. This act took effect in 1964. This act made **segregation** illegal and got rid of some practices that discriminated against African Americans.

Kennedy established the Peace Corps in 1961. This government-funded group sends trained American **volunteers** to other nations that need help.

IT'S A FACT!

IN 1961, PRESIDENT KENNEDY AND HIS BROTHER ROBERT, THE U.S. ATTORNEY GENERAL, SENT 600 FEDERAL MARSHALS TO ALABAMA TO PROTECT PEOPLE WHO WERE PROTESTING SEGREGATION. IN 1962, THEY SENT HUNDREDS OF FEDERAL OFFICERS TO PROTECT THE FIRST AFRICAN AMERICAN STUDENT TO ATTEND THE UNIVERSITY OF MISSISSIPPI.

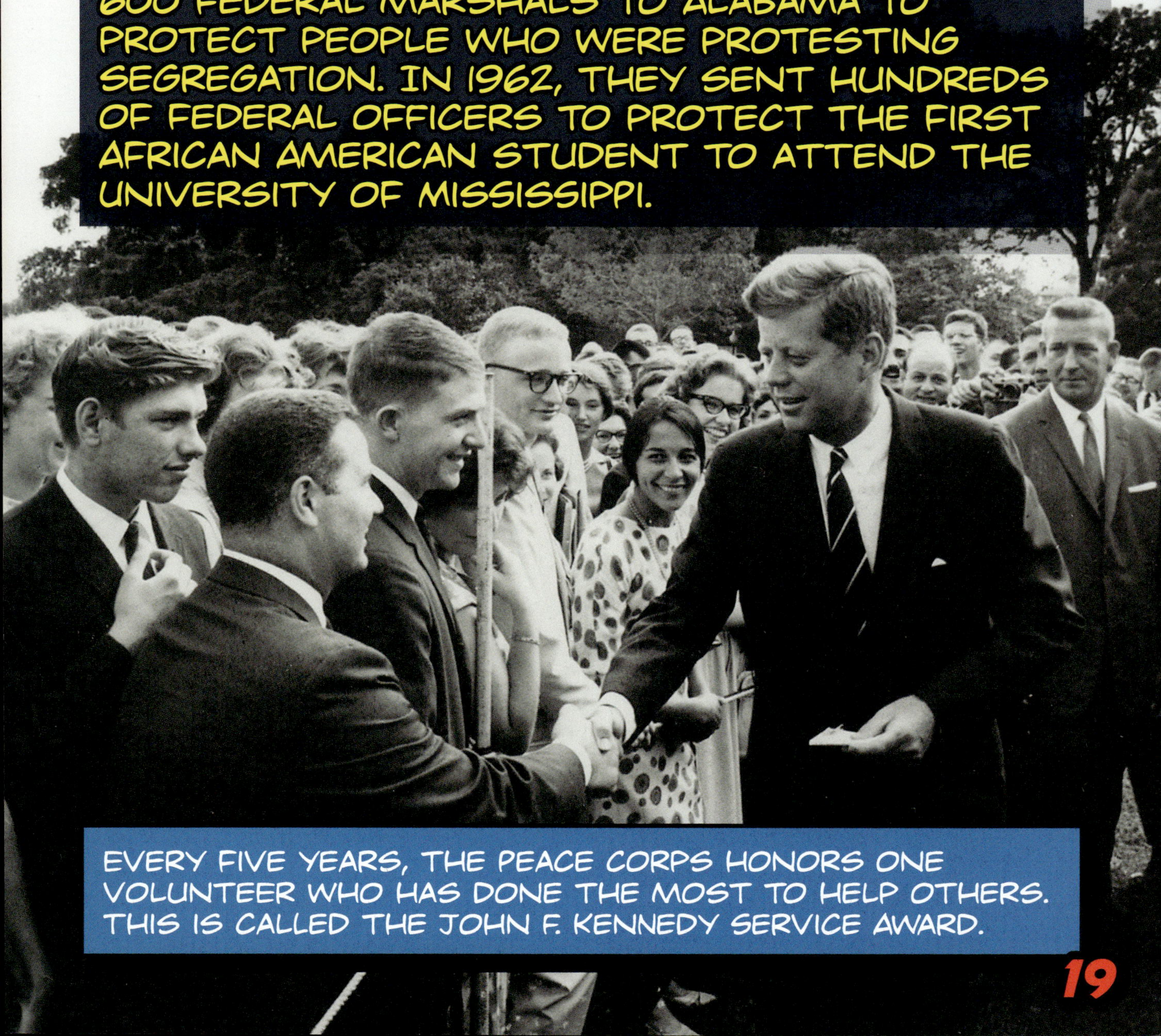

EVERY FIVE YEARS, THE PEACE CORPS HONORS ONE VOLUNTEER WHO HAS DONE THE MOST TO HELP OTHERS. THIS IS CALLED THE JOHN F. KENNEDY SERVICE AWARD.

A TRUE LEADER

Kennedy's assassination on November 22, 1963, was a sad moment for Americans. Today, most Americans think of Kennedy with respect. He fought for civil rights. He also fought to help the United States be the first nation to reach the moon! This is another feat that may never have occurred had it not been for Kennedy's leadership and vision.

Kennedy is buried in Arlington National Cemetery in Virginia. He received a very special honor. An "**eternal** flame" was placed above his grave.

KENNEDY'S TIMELINE

MAY 29, 1917	JOHN FITZGERALD KENNEDY IS BORN IN BROOKLINE, MASSACHUSETTS.
1936–1940	KENNEDY ATTENDS HARVARD UNIVERSITY.
1941	KENNEDY ENLISTS IN THE U.S. NAVY.
1942–1943	KENNEDY COMMANDS A PT BOAT IN THE SOUTH PACIFIC.
1946	KENNEDY IS ELECTED TO THE U.S. HOUSE OF REPRESENTATIVES.
1952	KENNEDY IS ELECTED TO THE U.S. SENATE.
SEPTEMBER 12, 1953	KENNEDY MARRIES JACQUELINE BOUVIER.
NOVEMBER 8, 1960	KENNEDY IS ELECTED PRESIDENT.
MARCH 1961	KENNEDY ANNOUNCES THE ESTABLISHMENT OF THE PEACE CORPS.
JUNE 1963	KENNEDY CALLS THE CIVIL RIGHTS STRUGGLE A "MORAL CRISIS" FOR AMERICA.
NOVEMBER 22, 1963	JOHN F. KENNEDY IS ASSASSINATED WHILE RIDING IN A CAR IN DALLAS, TEXAS. LYNDON JOHNSON BECOMES PRESIDENT.

GLOSSARY

activist: Someone who acts strongly in support of or against an issue.

Allies: The group of nations, including England and the United States, in World War II that opposed the Axis nations, including Germany and Japan.

assassinate: To kill someone, especially a public figure.

Civil Rights Act: An act passed in 1964 that outlawed segregation and discrimination based on race, color, religion, sex, and national origin.

communist: Having to do with communism, a system of government in which a single party controls state-owned means of production.

enlist: To enroll in the armed forces.

eternal: Lasting forever.

inauguration: A ceremonial induction into office.

intellectual: Having to do with the mind.

intelligence officer: A person in the military who collects, compares, and studies information.

last rites: In some Christian faiths, the prayers and rituals given to a person who is about to die.

oppression: Cruel or unjust use of authority or power.

philanthropy: A spirit of goodwill toward all people especially when expressed in active efforts to help others.

segregation: The separation of people based on race, class, sex, gender, or ethnicity.

volunteer: Someone who does something to help because they want to do it.

FOR MORE INFORMATION

BOOKS

Berglund, Bruce. *The Assassination of John F. Kennedy*. North Mankato, MN: Capstone Press, 2022.

Harrison, Wag. *The Presidents Did What?* Richmond, VA: Belle Isle Books, 2021.

Huddleston, Emma. *John F. Kennedy*. Mendota Heights, MN: North Star Editions, 2023.

WEBSITES

Biography: President John F. Kennedy
www.ducksters.com/biography/uspresidents/johnfkennedy.php
This website offers more information about the life and presidency of JFK.

John F. Kennedy
kids.nationalgeographic.com/history/article/john-f-kennedy
Read more about the life and death of President John F. Kennedy.

Publisher's note to educators and parents: Our editors have carefully reviewed these websites to ensure that they are suitable for students. Many websites change frequently, however, and we cannot guarantee that a site's future contents will continue to meet our high standards of quality and educational value. Be advised that students should be closely supervised whenever they access the internet.

INDEX